Strange Country

Also by Jon Thompson

POETRY
The Book of the Floating World
Landscape with Light

ESSAYS
Fiction, Crime and Empire
After Paradise: Essays on the Fate of American Writing

Jon Thompson

Strange Country

Shearsman Books

First published in the United Kingdom in 2016 by
Shearsman Books
50 Westons Hill Drive
Emersons Green
BRISTOL
BS16 7DF

Shearsman Books Ltd Registered Office
30–31 St. James Place, Mangotsfield, Bristol BS16 9JB
(this address not for correspondence)

www.shearsman.com

ISBN 978-1-84861-482-6

ACKNOWLEDGEMENTS
Heartfelt thanks to the editors of the following journals who published
the following poems:

Colorado Review: 'Deathward We Ride'; 'Paul Eluard Dreams of America'
Drunken Boat: 'Lavender Mist'; *Fortnightly Review*: 'Big Weather,'
'Lepanto,' 'LOL'; *Here/There*: 'When You Leave It All Behind'
Horizon Review: 'American Sublime'; *Mandala*: 'At The Ruins of the First
African-American Hospital Between Hampton, VA. and New Orleans,
LA., Founded in 1896, and Later Used As Part Of a State-Led Eugenics
Program'; *Mantis*: 'Finalsville'; *Molly Bloom*: 'It Broke from Within,'
'History. Desire. Tragedy. Repeat.';*Pangyrus*: 'To Paradise, I Give My Half-
Forgotten Dreams'; *Sixth Finch*: 'What They Believed'
The Other Room Anthology 7: 'Prequel,' 'Man Falling'; *Web Conjunctions*:
'White Light' ;*Word for Word*: 'Denny's'; 'Strange Fruit'; *Zone Poetry
Magazine*: 'History of the Twentieth Century,' 'Mega Millions'

Contents

1

II

For my mother, Claire Thompson,
who taught me to read.

"Poetry can repair no loss but it defies the space that separates. And it does this by its continual labor of reassembling what has been scattered."
—John Berger, *The Sense of Sight*

I

What They Believed

Some believed in a god that died for them.
Some believed that every day you need to
                        kill the god lodged in your heart.
Some believed god is an open window.
Some believed a storm is coming, that is why it is dark.

           •

Some believed the stars' flickering in the cold night sky is
                        an argument for a better self.
Some believed that love is older than the stars.
Some believed we are nothing but star dust.
Some believed dust is nothing but infinity made present.

           •

Some believed the self is something you become, like a sculpture
                        that finally finds its form.
Some believed the self is an unfinished sentence.
Some believed it was never more than a vanishing moon.
Some believed the self is one nation killing another.

           •

Some believed that the anger against the poor is a tide rising
                        that'll drown us all.
Some believed anger of the poor is a rising tide that'll drown us all.
Some believed justice is a riderless horse.
Some believed that the world is everything outside the house at
                        night with the TV on.

           •

Some believed violence is the mother we need to embrace.
Some believed it can be mined & refined, like a rare-earth metal.
Some believed it's a religion, to be honored with candles &
                    votive prayers.
Some believed there's a darkness in our hearts that demands the
                    death of those we hold most dear.

·

Some believed that trees secretly communicate with the wind.
Some believed that the polar caps are melting of their own accord.
Some believed that colors on a warm February day indicate
                    catastrophe.
Some believed, with sadness, that the world is all that is the case.

·

Some believed that dreams augur the future.
Some believed dreams are the ghosts of the past.
Some believed dreams are the stories you cannot bear to tell yourself
                    in the here-and-now.
Some believed that they must be murdered in their beds.

·

Some believed that the sun dreams of a different life, less
                    cataclysmic, less nuclear, less volatile.
Some believed that the sun is a sojourner, condemned to wander
                    in the silvery woods.
Some believed the sun is simply the sum of all of our desires.
Some believed the sun is a life-force whose life is half spent.

·

Some believed that you have to die to live.
Some believed that you have to live to die.
Some believed that living is dying, moment by moment.
Some believed that the only way to live is by distracting
                              yourself from the thought of dying.

                    •

Some believed poetry died a long time ago,
                    like epics, or astrolabes.
Some never thought of it at all.
Some heard in it voices that sang in their head.
Some believed it could awaken the dead.

Letter to Peter

As I write, it's summer & the spear-shaped leaves of the Japanese maple are tender with sunlight, which makes them luminous & almost transparent! Poetry, I believe, offers a language of apparition such that the Japanese maple in the poem can always be itself, but also betoken a pilgrimage on the way to something else, even if you're not sure where, or even, if you feel like going there. I like your eye, the way you use the knickknacks of Americana—like snow globes, for example—to register our strange childlike nature. In your poetry I hear a language alive to the white noise of our time, the vertigo of now. Your poems get lost in the bigness of the land & don't really try to find their way back. Peter, this is such a strange land, it needs a wide-open polyphony to capture it. Even artificial flowers possess a rare beauty, fake though they may be. Plastic bouquets on a white coffin are one of the saddest laments I know.

I like the way that trailer parks make their way into your poems, not as things, not even as places per se, but as zones of experience in which the TV is always on in front of couches that are worn out & scratched up, & hope isn't dead, but it's getting near the end. Hope that lives despite the non-transmission—or is it the non-reception?—of a snowy TV screen at 3.22 a.m. Because I find highways fascinating (they bring us past the banal & the sublime with such indifference!), I've been interested to see that you, too, are interested in them, especially signs by the side of the road, which are plainly declarative, but also misleading. They stand in your poems in all kinds of weather, except for snow. For some reason, road signs in your poems rarely have to contend with high drifts, or snow of any kind, which is a blessing, I suppose, but also mysterious as your poems are full of rain; rain that drenches, or at times, rain that falls softly like a blurred emotion, or rain heard from the warm inside of a house, with the musical patter of outsideness reminding one that while there is refuge, it's never complete.

Paul Eluard Dreams of America

I speak of cities

of imagined cities,
cities made from deepest desires,
cities early and late, unafraid
of excess, cities
unlike other cities,
cities without boundaries
shadowless under the sun.

Cities that dream and cry.

2.

A city is a kind of self
that invents itself.

A mask.

It deeply resembles you.

And you seem nothing like
a sky shivering with flashes of lightning.

You reveal yourself to yourself
to reveal yourself to others.

3.

Between the torments
between despair & the reason for living
there's injustice & this evil
that I can't accept.

I hear the fire talk of conscience.
I hear a man speak of what he has not known.

The fire is rising,
dying.

4.

Dreams in broad daylight
make the sun evaporate

make us cry, laugh
and cry.

Speak, then, dreams with nothing to say.

Make me speak of what is necessary to say.

5.

After years of assurance
during which the world was transparent

where then do

we think we are?

There are new words for cities
that've grown beyond our dreams.

6.

What's become of you   why this
solitude

which

we love to death?

A face like all the forgotten faces.

I said it to you for the clouds.

For the eye that becomes landscape or face.

I said it to you for your thoughts,
for your words.

7.

So many reasons to lose ourselves
on earth under horizon-less skies

under an exact goodness
that sets the earth in order.

I'm speaking to you now
of the living who resemble us.
All the living we fail to love.

Their lips tremble with joy
at the echo of leaden bells
at the muteness of beaten gold.
A lone heart   among other hearts

singing of the earth, as if it were ours.

LOL

If you can.
Funny that it is
all about an action
that's not happening.
Or is it an instruction
to find the world funny?
How funny
is that. World, world
of code & semaphore,
messages that blink
for a bit & then
are gone, like an
SOS with only
the faintest, most
hidden, of
distress signals.

Mega Millions

About the living having
available to them
all manner of hope: the
promise of
nothing less than
the transformation of
the self beyond self, the
very sequence of
daily life brought to
plenitude & fulfillment.
After so many near
misses, it seems
only fair for there finally
to be compensation for the
oversights; walking through
the isles of brightly-colored products
I think, this
is what I want:
to have the Megaplier
redress the multiplied
omissions & bring
balance to the world.
The minutiae of individual
experience converted into
vastness, an incontestable
richness no extended calculus
could take away.

Report from I-85, Middle of the Week, Middle of My Life

A certain boredom with
roads leading to
other roads, highways leading
to other highways; distances
marked by green interstate signs
& big-box agglomerations that
might've, in another age,
become towns. Size
is what we do.
The instead-of,
the-in-place-of, are
not remarkable. We do
towns without towns,
cities without cities.
You, my heart, are
a multiplex on the way
to becoming a megalopolis.
The weather's indifferent;
traffic's pretty much
the same. Ersatz
emotion pours out of
the evangelical radio station
as you blow past
brightly-lit franchise signs
on kudzu-covered hills…

Big Weather

Low hum or high winds,
hard to say. Outsideness
looks cinematic,
the world putting on airs
with winter-stripped trees,
gospel-swaying back & forth
outside old-fashioned paned glass.
Winter-sharp branches
wave wildly,
sough a song not their own.
Wrens try out a call &
response in the
emptiness between
boughs then
wing away. What
is the weather?
It's mainly a feeling,
a set of feelings
that defines a day.
A happening that causes panic;
a happening instead of panic.
In the place of clouds,
an exilic grey mass is moving
eastward, pushing light out of the way.
There's a travelling in the air,
an ideation & dispossession
that's premonitory,
a sense of something coming,
something you have not agreed to.
A quietness. A waiting for catastrophe,
or a waiting that does without it.

Suburban Estate Sale

Faded red & gold 1939 USC Rose Bowl banner; red & white 1959 LA Dodgers National League Champions banner; one small porcelain figurine of a peasant girl, sitting brookside, with pink peasant dress & white headscarf, mass produced; dachshund salt & pepper shakers; stainless steel saucepans piled up on the stove; hospital-green Tupperware containers; shoebox full of pristine German beer-mats; Tyrolese walking shorts, jacket & homburg; one dark-brown wooden American eagle, wall-mounted; cast-iron cornbread mold in the shape of 6 shucked corn-on-the cobs; assorted white crockery; set of four white teacups with saucers; five Russian-looking gold-and-black teacups with saucers; collection of German beer mugs and glasses with embossed beer brands; soft marionette dolls of Adolf Hitler & Eva Braun, looking heroic; small porcelain figurine collection including a cowboy holding a guitar with brown cowboy boots, an Alaskan Eskimo woman in quasi-Alaskan gear with heavily mascaraed eyelashes, an Andean native with red-knit shawl, and a pig standing up in Scottish plaids with a tam o shanter at a cocky angle; heavily-used, thickly-padded black leather La-Z-Boy; six dachshunds of various sizes and materials, some cast-iron black, some smaller ones done in brass; one brown & tan porcelain dachshund on the mantel; set of four Gorham steak knives; various cook books including *The ABC of Barbecue* and *Easy to Make Maidens & Cocktails*; a Silex Juicit juicing machine; an unused, still-in-the-box GE Custom Portable Mixer; a Jelco Eddie 8mm film editor; a JVC boombox; a cycling machine; a box of 1959 Dodgers White Sox programs; half a dozen hand-carved, hand-painted wooden ducks; silver teaspoon collection mounted in a blue velvet case; vintage Norwegian skis; Topps Baseball Stamp Album; poster of triumphant 19th century suffragette in the *Onward Victoria* musical; collection of costume jewelry necklaces & bracelets in the upstairs bedroom; white plastic mannequin head, female, on make-up table with heavy black aviator sunglasses & an unused wig, tawny brown, styled in a bob.

Denny's

Red letters on a yellow sign
can be more than friendly,
as can outsized plastic menus
& brown imitation-leather
naugahyde the air is bright
with chatter & the clatter of
plates & silverware it's
corporate-friendly &
focus-group tested, customer-
relations approved—utterly
lacking in charm but
happy in a standardized
American postsomething way.
The mind wants to feel that
experience is unique but
what if it isn't? Denny's is
the cheerful acceptance of
that fact. I'm working on
acceptance in a clean,
well-lighted place, sunlight is
streaming through the window
with the highway outside it
leading to other highways,
other Denny's—Dear Reader,
everything here says, give
up on mimesis, on the spell of
the unique. Live under
the spell of seriality,
one thing after the other.

Cell Tower Utopia

Bristling with accoutrement, it
bounces words across
space. The spectral
"A," is a bad mini Eiffel Tower.
At dusk, it contrasts with
the pink summer sky like
a structure from an early
twentieth-century sci-fi fantasy,
emitting intermittent icy-blue
blinking lights, clumsily futuristic.
Spiky brethren everywhere.
It makes the voices of the
living ghostly present. Come down,
come down all ye voices
& live with the living for
a while. Forget the chatter of this & that,
the traffic of fear, bad feelings,
worse selves. Enter the mess of
the here-and-now. The kingdom
you speak of is not there.

American Sublime

Midnight on Park Avenue: the night purple-black
but clear, the cold invigorating with a hint of spring
in it. Pedestrians enjoying the air, the relief from the
showers, a spirit of camaraderie abroad as they spill
out of restaurants & take to the streets, reluctant
to let go of the night. Walking up Park Avenue,
the eye is drawn to the Chrysler building, its lit-up
chrome crown & spire swathed in gauzy clouds—
impossible sight!—the extravagant art deco design,
the terraced arches and triangular windows a
cathedral to an older modernity full of light &
grace, a salute to the sublime still unsurpassed, &
the outcropping big-beaked eagles the American
version of gargoyles so fierce they appear to monitor
the movements of the city below—the silver eagles,
the skyscraper, capitalism itself a chimera radiant in
the night.

Deathward We Ride

In Memoriam W.G. Sebald

Deathward we ride
improvising our way
but the white door that opens history
opens onto wetlands flooded
with dreams of floods
handwritten fragments from
a forgotten past the
lost manuscripts of simple
hopes the revelation that "this happened
and this happened" & then
death—it's as if
the photograph of that time was overexposed
but instead of sepia-yellow
an unearthly pink tints the image of
ruins
rising barely above the water
strange that the village on the coastline
would be rebuilt again and again
across the centuries
after being
swallowed up
again and again
the ocean that crashes onto the beach
at night is terribly black
but the surf is white brilliantly deathly white
a surging that takes itself
closer and closer to the dim low
white settlement in the distance

Lepanto

And did those in the warship with the long oars

see

the defeat in the triumph

on the long odyssey home?

The childish scrawl gives the galley a gaiety

                                        & an innocence.

An outline of triumph against the elements, buoyant blue.

The wind flutters the banners. Oars dig deep.

The world lies before it: everything to be won.

But something else

in the banners' jubilant waving.

Lepanto Lepanto Lepanto:

the letters & sounds are running backward

after Cy Twombly's drawings

It Broke from Within

after Ai Weiwei's 'Marble Chair'

Say a famous artist made a life-sized yoke-back chair out of the finest Italian marble, with a russet stain that spreads from spindle to seat like a greedy flame.

Imagine the famous artist's father was a poet whose whispered last words were: "Imagine, a white marble chair…"

Say the famous artist came from a country of tyrants, & as a child his family was forced into exile & of all their possessions, they were allowed to keep only a yoke-back chair, much like the marble chair. How, then, would you regard the marble chair?

Say the artist never touched the chair, just imagined it, and handed off its production to paid-by-the-hour artisans. Would you call it his?

Imagine not one marble chair, but a cavernous hall full of them, lined up in symmetrical rows, hundreds of them there with an oddly expectant air…

Say one of the marble chairs was purchased by a museum in the American Midwest, in a city famous for its museums, where the room in which it was exhibited was never visited, never seen. Would the marble chair then be an inferior work of art—or would it belong to a superior class, of a category not yet named or conceived?

Say the dust from the cutting, carving and the sanding of the marble calcified the lungs of the artisans & made their bodies cold as stones in winter. How, then, would you regard the marble chair?

Say you found out that the dictator ritualistically ordered the death of dissidents and artists, bound & gagged in the chair before an audience of other artists & dissidents, making their death a grotesque spectacle of blood running down the white marble chair. How, then, would you regard the chair?

Say, alternately, that the dictator so hated the marble chair that he forced the imprisoned artist to witness its destruction blow by blow until there was nothing but polished shards. Would he have destroyed the marble chair?

Imagine an American poet preoccupied by the chair. He writes a prose poem about it. One day a memory comes to him from childhood. He realizes that the marble chair is associated in his mind with Mass, with the large, imposing altar chair the priest would sit in. When the priest stood to bless the Host, the tortured body of God's son hung on a crucifix above the throne-like chair, & although he now knows Christ's body was not carved, was factory made, he remembers three tear-shaped, scarlet-red drops of blood painted on his beige, spiked feet. Since that god lives for him only as a memory, what strikes him most about the marble chair now is its emptiness, the summoning of an authority that isn't there. O the melancholia of the marble chair!

Voices in Our Heads
That Are Also Everywhere

What
we cannot do
without: that voice
& its never-ending how.
Surely no surer way
to undo all the
compromised arrangements
than that. On
one day the prescription
is X & another it's Y.
When you wake
to that day when
you have to kill
the thing you love,
when you wake
to the dread that
you will have
to kill the thing that
you love, & then
you do it, time
slows & the
greenness in the leaves
seems to exceed
their appointed shape
& the day
seems longer than
it should &
what's left tastes
bitter. It turns out
it's always time
to say goodbye,

but when you do
the voices of instruction
are there, too,
in their banality,
their one-shot deal
that shape-shifts
into another one,
but it's wrong to
blame them because
it's we who summon
them. When you
think of it,
it's heartbreaking
that we demand voices
that twist us up
& ravage the lives
we could've had,
so it's necessary to
bury the thought that
"I could've had this."
The undead take
so much energy to
keep down. The
iterations become
endless, the drama
a grim play of
inventiveness. I'd
like so much
to tell you
how to escape them, or
how to silence them,
but then I'd
be one of them.
But you can still
witness

the fused force
of greenness
that renders
the seen world
incomprehensible,
witness the beauty
that makes
apparitional
the terrible voices
that don't even exist.

When You Leave It All Behind

There's no sadness like that of an American strip mall, slowly
dying.

Plastic teal-green roofs of unvisited stores sing
of the simple life, neo-real.

Acres of washed-out asphalt w/ white diagonal parking-lot lines.

Hum of the beltline fading in & out.

Rusting light poles support stiff red white & blue "Welcome"
banners.

It's patriotic to by-pass a long, slow death like this.

And the summer sky can't help it; it's a picture-perfect, light-blue,
still
in high advertisement mode.

Even the discounted dread the long, slow transmogrification.

All this non-place, non-bustle, tick of long seconds, filling up space.

O my sad captain, this is what we've done.

> What is it we wanted?
> Something that was here.

Circa Now

after Cesar Vallejo

No one lives there anymore—the neighbors all know it.
The living room, the bedrooms, the kitchen live in silence.
The patio, open to the sun, is deserted. Nobody's here; they've
                                                        all left.

The standard still-lifes are still hanging
on the walls. Framed photographs of children haunt the empty
                                                        spaces.
Dresser drawers are half-open with clothes spilling out.

A sadness & a humiliation, perfectly preserved. Footsteps have
                                        fled, & kisses,
ordinary pardons & ordinary crimes. Everything as in some
                                        latter-day museum, but
not. Everything swept; clean. Living on: the negation, loudest
                                        of assertions.

"South of the Border"

Billboards straight out of
1950s Americana live
on in the borderlands.
It's instructive to see
how a nation dreams.
There's nothing here
that cries "beware!,"
"beware!" but
unselfconsciousness
has its own perils. Hello
muzack, kitsch &
kiddieland joy. Hello
fireworks. Pedroland's decked
out in green, white & red
stripes. Hello WASP mind
seeing itself in funhouse
mirrors & finding it funny.
Hello Pleasure Dome
of no decree, you're now
grimy, but at least
there's no holy dread.
You hope, not for
a miracle, but for some
plausibly semi-rare device.
Not paradise, but at least
not a place where its
absence will be
bitter to see.

Watching Cage Fighting on Pay Per View

Our gaze leads us
to this theater.

Our being is
here.

We want to take
in the drama.

We want
victory.

The victor is the one who will
sustain the most damage.

Once there was a boy lost
& looking for pride.

Once there was a world
outside the cage.

Strange Fruit

> The "I" in the mode of knowing, knows
> its own vulnerability, and thus others.'

How exquisite the
thinking behind
this thought, like
ruins not yet ruins.
And of vulnerability,
mine, dense as the
blackness outside my
window, nightsong
darkness no song
throbbing out there
beyond the glass but
some kind of
unidentifiable subtonal
thrum—life thrum, death
thrum, who can
say?—but does knowing
oneself, knowing
others mean seeing
the vulnerability
in others? I speak
only out of
my own vulnerability.
Every individual,
every epoch, shelters
its abject darkness,
its unspeakable
counter-arguments.
Perhaps the "I"
that comes to
know its own

terrible vulnerability also
comes to see, comes
to know, the
vulnerability of
others—but is
unmoved, unchanged
by that recognition.
That's a farness
you don't want
to push past. A
god of another
self, unpropitiated
by small sacrifices.

History, Desire, Tragedy. Repeat.

The landscape repeats itself as flat
& featureless until you reach the foothills
& it's after history with the long perspective
of afternoon light traveling along
a winter's day, cut only by
a flat black strip of highway, without snow.
Then there's the story of the crushing weight
of failure day after day, unavoidable
as the mountains, which are
terrible in their beauty (in the distance
the snowy peaks are rose & salmon-tinted,
with the sun diffused through
an alchemy of clouds). In the
wind noise, you hear rumors
of more wars, negotiations, broken
truces, but with all the evidence of the past
cleared away, it's hard to take them in,
in part because it's the third cycle of
the third era & all the photographs
of men in uniforms in strange lands
are dog-eared & oddly familiar & in the wind rush
you can still hear the keening
of women in black robes
alongside a highway that repeats itself
in a mantra of emptiness.

In Memoriam

] Afghanya   ] Al Qaim   ] Alasay

] Azizabad   ] Baghdad   ] Baqubah   ] Basra

] Chora   ] Dahneh   ] Fallujah   ] Haditha

] Husaybah   ] Kamdesh   ] Kamdin   ] Kandahar

] Kanez   ] Kunduz   ] Karbala   ] Mazari Sharif

] Mosul   ] Najaf   ] Nasiriyah   ] Nasrat

] Ramadi   ] Samarra   ] Sangin   ] Shah Wali Kat

] Takur Ghar   ] Tal Afar   ] Tora Bora   ] Turki

] Umm Qasr

] Fallujah] Fallujah]Fallujah

II

Orange Alert

Throngs float through giant concourses in orchestrated silence.

All the airport signs are now in a strange alphabet, perhaps Cyrillic?

Faces of calm repose.

Shiny advertisements belonging to the school of the New Pastoralism.

Moving sidewalks take you past fantastic paintings.

Moving sidewalks take you past screens with skyscrapers on fire.

Airport personnel are now x-raying bones.

In the Lost & Found, mountains of suitcases with no owners.

Banality more memorable than you can endure.

Your destination is a piece of paper you hold in your hand.

Your destination is a country with no past.

Exiled deep in the heart, fear's the new passport.

Watching the Evening News

Strange the syllables we mimic to shape the world.

Terror of not being a number, one of the uncounted, the un–.

Voices like prayers or psalms rising above the smoke of burning pyres.

White mountains, like fissured fables, fall into the sea.

Things that are happening will happen to you too.

Minor Incident at the End of a War

1.

For five years he'd dreamt of many things, but had stopped dreaming of this: of a chopper that'd whisk him away from the forested ridges and valleys of Paktika Province which would show a land shaped like opened palms in prayer. Once rescued, he spoke of many privations, including a five-month spell in an iron cage in complete darkness, where he was fed monkey meat & for companionship had only the trills and whistles of a nightingale. In his dreams, men in pearl-grey shalwar kameezes rode white horses through the fields of Idaho at dawn, trampling high stalks under sharp hooves, but in those dreams, those he loved had disappeared from the earth; when the Afghanis galloped off, there was only the fluted sound of the wind through the wheat.

2.

One military inquiry said the American soldier simply deserted his post, disappearing into the dusty backcountry without a trace. One (buried) report outlined a breakdown of military discipline on the remote post leading him to become disillusioned with the casual brutality of his comrades, who it was said, would run over Afghani children in Army trucks for sport; in this same report, it was also noted he had begun to learn Pashto & to spend his free time with Afghanis, and being unable to abide the hypocrisy of the occupation any longer, one evening it seems he just walked off. To be captured. One fellow soldier said he was "weird" because he read a lot. One testified to him being a straight-up guy. Another found it troubling he'd spend time tracing ancient trading routes with his forefinger over old maps of Afghanistan and Pakistan. Another claimed that he found him at dusk one evening in an area far from base talking to an enormous fig tree in which dozens and dozens of songbirds had congregated, all singing back to him songs of unearthly beauty.

3.

On the day he returned home, he was rushed to a military prison. In the tomb-like darkness of his cell he dreamed again of Idaho, this time he saw open sage and grass fields, unfolding in a long dusk light. No people. It was if there had never been people. The light on the land had a rare clarity, richer for the imminence of its extinction. Above, dark clouds massing in the expanse of the sky, were not symbolic; they were just intensely meteorological, actual in their real-time formation. Once massed, they look like the low mountains brooding in the distance. In the dream, the openness was vast & epoch-old, possessing a kind of terrible freedom, like every hope you ever had, fulfilled.

Man Falling

To take the hymn of the world from the world, you need a
                                                    brutal heart.

The sun rolls across the sky, routinely non-apocalyptic
        in its run-through of works & days.
        No running out of dreams, no terror of the shadow
        on the shadow, the slow march across the sundial...

A thousand mirrors. A thousand fires,
        a thousand slow declensions
        a thousand visions imprisoning the un-tragedy
        of long-dead dramas flaring into life.

"Eyes as windows..." That's what he remembered
        as he fell through the flames, the sound of the wind,
the sound of the world, rushing
        like words he could not hear.

A Brief History of the Twentieth Century

L., the main character in the novel titled *L* by Georg Lukács, is the story of a Hungarian revolutionary whose life is marked by upheaval and scholarship, sometimes conducted under strained circumstances. Born to an investment banker, L. gains a reputation for himself as a political theorist who, among other things, writes famous, if controversial, books under different names. His novel, which contemporary readers have all but forgotten, details L.'s life and times in Central Europe in a post-WWI world fractured by fiercely-competing socialist sects and purges. In a manuscript version of the novel, his protagonist becomes a Commissar in Hungary during the period of the short-lived Hungarian Soviet Republic. In a particularly charged scene, L. executes eight people in Poroszló in May of 1919. It's not clear from the language whether the executed were partisans on L's side of the conflict who had somehow betrayed the cause, or whether they were enemies in the conflict who were being punished for simply being enemies. The language in this part of the novel makes interpretation difficult inasmuch as it tightly focuses upon the physical movements of L. leading up to the execution itself, and the detail is so sharply delineated it possesses an almost hallucinatory power. Some scholars see suggestions that the execution is motivated by a desire to punish war-time atrocities. This interpretation is debatable, however, because it hinges on a single word, the word for "prisoner," which can be translated variously, each interpretation implying a different level of culpability. The final version of the novel, disappointingly, eliminates the important scene entirely: after a brief period of imprisonment, the prisoners are pardoned and allowed, in the interests of rebuilding society, to return to their homes. Reviewers found this section of the novel to be the weakest. In its time, however, the novel was a great success. It blended a skillful pacing of the plot with elements of suspense, and surprisingly, elements of the fantastic. For example, Thomas

Mann, a friend of L.'s, gives him papers that renders anyone encountering him incapable of recalling his true identity and his past, and armed with these papers, L. is able to elude the police and slip out of many difficult situations as he flees to the Soviet Union. In the Soviet Union, however, the papers lose their magical properties and he is caught up in the Great Terror and, along with the exemplary figure of David Riazanov, L. is forced into a kind of in-house arrest working as an archivist in the library in the basement of the Marx-Engels Institute in Moscow. The narrator makes much of the oppressive weight of the snow on the candy-colored onion domes and spires of the Kremlin as a parallel to the confinement of these underground men. One particularly powerful scene describes L. coming across an unknown letter from Marx to his house-keeper/mistress, Helen Demuth, regarding their illegitimate child, in which he describes at great length his passion for Helen and his great guilt at allowing his son to be put out at a working-class foster home in London to be trained as a tool-maker. The novel zeroes in upon the ethical quandary L. faces, the moral and political dilemma he must negotiate, as he contemplates saving Marx's reputation by destroying the letter or, alternately, being true to history by allowing the letter to exist, but, in so doing, clouding Marx's reputation. (In the end, L. does neither: he does not inform Riazanov of the document, but neither does he destroy it, but instead he secretes it into the back of a little-read file). Riazanov thus emerges as the moral center of the novel. Fingered by an assistant who was tortured into identifying Riazanov as leading a counter-revolutionary Menshevik conspiracy, he is forced to submit to a show trial, and is immediately executed after refusing to implicate anyone else in the trumped-up case. One of the finest passages in the novel, and one of its final ones, is a small masterpiece of dark surrealism: Lukács describes the wolves of Russia keening together throughout that cold, cloud-shredded, moon-lit night in collective protest over the execution. Realism: powerless in the face of the grotesquerie of the world.

Train Through a Southern Landscape

Darkness as not-day, palpable
in its negation. Nothing
for the eye to rest
upon, nothing to distract
the mind from its unavoidable
reckonings. In the distance
the long moan of a freight train—
less moan than admonition—
rumbles through the night,
all motion and vibration
filling the darkness, obligato
of the past joining
the train's deep-bassed
declarations. We cannot see
what we cannot see.
Windows are blank eyes.
All the old uncertainties,
all the old doubts, appear
as indisputable facts. In the
dark, half-remembered
footnotes to history feel
closer, nearer. It's the work,
the work! You hear the unceasing
work of commerce driving
past as a succession that's
unslowable. Its sound: pure
sadness. It makes the night night.

At the Ruins of the First African-American Hospital Between Hampton, Va. and New Orleans, La., Founded in 1896, and Later Used As Part of a State-Led Eugenics Program

Silence in the place of silence.
A cheap chain-link fence holds it in.
Now and then the creak of a yellow traffic light
swinging in the wind. Through the roofless,
windowless stone-and brick walls, you
can see the bitter loss, the sharp azure-blue sky
big beyond belief, promising nothing. What
goodness, what atrocity, happened here.
Ruin as non-memorial, commemorating nothing.
Winter-whitened Bermuda grass surviving, the
end prophetic. The old oak next to the nailed-in
front doors a witness to
every parade of hope & pain.
No words to hold on to.

Reflecting on a Pain in the Body
That Finally Arrived in This Poem

Begin with the word
& hope to find its promise:

breaths taken & held,
for memory, new territory—

until now, there was not that word—and now
like breath comes in the

half-empty shining:
a still incomprehensible prayer

(as for a child).
Realm of the broken

where the breath
is taken & held.

The light that fell fell
diagonally across

the field, winter-bright, the room
curtained, divided against

the blankness of days.
Fables of new beginnings.

Fables of what
you will be.

No answer
to the question, what

shall be commensurate
with what?

Anti-Dithyrambic

Indifferent clarity of a winter day:
sunlight warming the ground, blue sky
arching overhead in a mockery
of the very idea of day. Beat down
of a chopper's rotor blades traversing
the condition of now. Afterwash of sound,
then nothing. To have come this far without
knowing why or what for, knowing
the question is itself a presumption. After a
time, consciousness is a condensation
of questions; the trees, shorn
of leaves, are outside the weariness of words.
Sunlight warms the washed-out, grey-black
asphalt, the street's smooth surface; shadows
cast by stripped tree branches dance
in the street, then stop. Gradually,
the hieroglyphs thin out & disappear.

Prequel

To be here
in sight of
the infinite play
of water & clouds—
is to be in
a rhythm of
endlessness
like the refrain
of the surf—to be
in that
place and to feel
the moment, lotioned
innocence, is, also,
to feel
it draining
away, as an age
that's coming
to an end,
& there's nothing
for it; it will
leave you, you
will leave it,
the loneliness
in the knowledge
of it not being
endless equal
only to the loneliness
of its larger
endlessness,
the larger span
behind it, nonhuman
time in which cliff rock

gets ground up
a millennium or two
later deposited here as a
white stretch of sand,
warming under
a June sun, there
for the pleasure
of those who,
so gifted, approach
the surf after
it has stretched up
to the driest
part of the beach,
reflecting in its short-lived
sheeted shimmer
an amortized sky,
a glimpse
permitted before
it's withdrawn,
leaving the great
heaving Atlantic
out there
indifferent in its
massive, dark-
hued beauty.

Triptych: In a Country Beyond Naming

I

Lavender Mist

Not just frequency but duration—
everything a convergence, a working towards & a working out

        things repeat themselves again and again
but they're different, as the light is different from day to day,
        brighter, more brilliant
more declarative, urgent, rarer
        enlivening the least of things,
the unasked-for second chance—
the world in its stillness, still a singular gift
        never held out for long.

At other times, it's Sunday-somber,
dimly sacramental,
sacrificial
        whistled through with a pain so huge
you can't see how the world could stand it
fading soft and mournful
        —silent dirge—

In the painting, the thin black strokes are men
striding through
        a city of cross purposes.
Each is moving toward a different future
        making & moving away from
the hubbub of motion & energy & light they're trying to leave
behind.
Although you have to imagine it, a fine lavender mist is falling
everywhere.

II
White Light

After all the fear & desire—
parabolic curves
of the mind that
feels itself
    part of the labyrinth & not.
Double-consciousness, double-vision, double-takes:
         nervous tics

of the one-eyed, evidence
of compulsive iteration.

"Our machinery was devastating.
And versatile. It could do everything
but stop."

Strange light for a strange world,
      sidereal, surreal, solid
it ushers in a new connectedness,
the feathery blackness of white, the feathery whiteness of black,
last glimpses of
a country beyond naming.

III
One

Rage: the plain desire for it to be cleansed
                                    by lines that sweep

insouciantly
up to heaven's face, showing

an equipoise in the light,
                          the clear midsummer light,
that here & there makes itself felt before

giving way to the terrible darkness,
                              the terrible arterial beauty
that's bleeding away.

TV Nation

All day, all night, screens glow with silvery poise.

Flickerings from scene to scene, undaunted by the absence
of viewers.

Babble of voices, insistent in their tinny theatricality.

I can't seem to get at the feeling, not loneliness
but some sadness beyond it.

Digitized non-loneliness, non-sadness, glowing in the dark.

The World, The Text, The Poem

The ruins of memory
in the rubble of tomorrow, tomorrow & tomorrow.

The shattering itself epic,
cathedral-like & silent, with

violent up-thrusts into air.
Nowhere the angel of possibility.

The long solitary door is
locked at the end of the hall—

all the doors we can't go through
and behind them, the gift of light,

seventeenth-century, Vermeer-thick &
varnished with the patina of another age, is

radiant with a richness
free from contemplation.

To Paradise, I Give My Half-Forgotten Dreams

I.

So this is
it. Is it
singular in itself
still, whole, inviolate
despite the many
depredations? You can
see slender branches
waving gently in
the dispensation of
the wind, ignorant
of all but
the essential. The
rustle of lightness
stirs the world.
Though few believe
it, there's no
sin. Unspeakable atrocity
yes; ordinary cruelties,
yes; but no
sin. Even now,
the world's impossibly
verdant & self-possessed.
In the whisperings
of a late autumnal
light, the pure
weight, the inertia,
the opacity of
the past, seems
like a distant
memory no longer

capable of arrowing
you. But that
you will be
arrowed is inescapable.
That's the deal:
beauty holds out
many promises, many
balms, but it will
not save you.

II

Here, of course,
it's only beauty
that can save you.
But salvation does
not come without
cost. Its uncanniness
must be lived,
thrilling, but deeply
uncomfortable, like visiting
a museum with
room after room
open to the sky,
full of streaming
sunlight, in
which paintings of
inexpressible beauty
just by being there
indict a lesser world.
Or when taking
a walk &
seeing—still alive!—
the artless, simple
Painted Trillium,

the simple Star
of Bethlehem, the
yellow & white
Alium, the violet
yellow & white
Dwarf Crested Iris,
testaments to
the flagrant beauty
we live with
without regard for
its delicate, salvational
force. True beauty,
it turns out,
is unendurable. Its
promise is too
painful, too immense
to rise to, the
possibilities too frightening.
It is comforting,
instead, to render
the world ugly,
beyond redemption. Here
paradise is the
unconsciousness, unknowable
but silently
framing what's possible.
How many other
civilizations have
achieved our level
of despoliation, our
unregenerate ugliness?
We've replaced the
real with the
destructiveness
of the ideal.

The need to
forget then triumphs
over the imperative
to change. In
paradise, tragedies cannot
ever be seen.

III

In paradise, wants
& needs become
indistinguishable, making
it the culmination
of generations of
confused desire. Each
desire becomes layered
with new generations of
desire making it
palimpsestic. Therefore, the
culmination of everything
to be feared.
I want, for instance,
not an end
to the tawdry, but
a limit. I want
the feeling of
American vastness to
be accompanied by
intimacy. I want streets
of a new
dawn, not closed-
down glamour avenues
of dusk, the shopfront
displays radiant with
expense. I want

clocks in public
places with hands
that will go
backwards stopping
at moments of
singular possibility,
just to remember
what that is
like. I want
death to not be
a corrupt stranger.
I want cities
in which
art is more
than proof of
grotesque wealth. I
want all the old
grand dreams of
the avant-garde
to be as
common & actual
as trash. I
want the ruins we
created honored
with pilgrimages.
I want trash
everywhere
to be luminous.

IV

Paradise means fear.
Fear that someone
will take it
away. Fear that

it was not
what was desired;
fear that it
will not be
what was desired.
Fear that what
is beautiful will
be subtracted from
your life, too.
Fear that it
is as beautiful as
it seems. A
nation can fantasize,
but fear &
desire start with
individuals. And what
you fear, you
can desire &
what you desire,
you'll always fear.
To live in
paradise means
accepting a high
degree of vulnerability
as the defining
condition of your
life. To be
vulnerable without ever
being able to
admit it is
to be condemned
to living a
kind of double
life, lived &
passed from generation

to generation, an inescapable
inheritance, unspoken but
expressed in the
language of gesture,
especially in our
fearful violence, which
despite its abject
unboundedness, is always,
among other things,
an unacknowledged plea
for forgiveness.

V

If I could remember
the scene completely
it'd be something
like this: evening,
and being
stuck on a highway
with hundreds of
other cars stopped
in traffic. But
the light, the
light was dazzling,
a glinting that
came from a
thousand reflections
shimmering off
glassfronts, a rejoinder
to the sun, less
the light of
transcendence & more
a reply to
nature, a testament

to what is, what
isn't now
possible, as when
the traffic moved
again, & the
unified shimmer disappeared
& the moment
returned to the
quotidian, the
terror not in
the moment of
a thousand windshields
flickering & glinting,
but in the
banality of the
big-box chain-
stores that lined the
highway with all
the signs
pointing to other
signs, indifferent to
any other transaction.

Finalsville

Now that all the songs have been sung, now
that the wind is barely a memory over what were once fields,

now that the earth refuses to bequeath more secrets,
silence will be the epochal sound

of the land. All the long-gone
civilizations will exist in that sound.

All the different words for the same
things will co-exist & expire

in the cessation of that breath.
The earth will be the unrecorded

expression of its own being. Birch forests,
silvery in the shadows, will be the new alphabet.

For Nick Halpern

Notes

'Letter to Peter' is addressed to Peter Gizzi.

'South of the Border' is a tourist trap/fireworks and souvenir outlet in South Carolina close to the border between South Carolina and North Carolina. It's known for its many garish billboards.

'Strange Fruit': The lines "The 'I' in the mode of knowing, knows/its own vulnerability, and thus others'" are from Peter Riley's *Due North*.

'Orange Alert' is a response to a poem by Kazim Ali by the same name. My poem adapts a line from Franz Wright's 'East Window: Little Compton' in *Wheeling Motel* : "Though soon//things as they are will become far/more memorable than you can endure."

'Triptych: In a Country Beyond Naming': the following sentences are from Michael Herr's *Dispatches*: "Our machinery was devastating. And versatile. It could do everything but stop."

Lastly, thanks to family, friends & generous souls along the way who have offered various forms of support: Jennifer Atkinson, Barbara Baines, Dan Beachy-Quick, Molly Bendall, David Blakesley, Aisling Chester, Catherine Chester, Suzanne Chester, Sofie Chester-Thompson, Zoe Chester-Thompson, Matthew Cooperman, Kelvin Corcoran, Angela Davis-Garner, Leigh DeNeef, Elizabeth Goizueta, Roberto Goizueta, Giles Goodland, Carolyn Guinzio, Nick Halpern, Brenda Hillman, Aby Kaupang, Peter Kline, Lew Klatt, Elizabeth Kunreuther, Chris Kondrich, Alexander Levy, India Levy, Pelham Levy, Megan Horstmann, Agnes Lehoczky, Thomas Lisk, Aisling Maguire, Richard Marshall, Leila May, Bill McQuade, Jason Miller, Patricia Morgado, Elaine Orr, Don Palmer, Eric Pankey, Agustin Pasten, Brittany Perham, Adam Piette, Ethel Rackin, Peter Riley, Aidan Semmens, Sharon Setzer, Laura Severin, Simon Smith, Joe Thompson, Mike Thompson, Sara Thompson, Daniel Tiffany, Chris Tonelli, and Keith Tuma. And, of course, thanks to Tony Frazer for making *Strange Country* a book.

CPSIA information can be obtained
at www.ICGtesting.com
Printed in the USA
FSOW01n0013090916
24698FS